D0759745

STEGOSAURUS

By Brian Thomas

Gareth Stevens
PUBLISHING

leveled
reader
science

Please visit our website, www.garethstevens.com. For a free color catalog of all our high-quality books, call toll free 1-800-542-2595 or fax 1-877-542-2596.

Library of Congress Cataloging-in-Publication Data

Thomas, Brian.
Stegosaurus / by Brian Thomas.
p. cm. — (A look at dinosaurs)
Includes index.
ISBN 978-1-4824-1827-9 (pbk.)
ISBN 978-1-4824-1825-5 (6-pack)
ISBN 978-1-4824-1826-2 (library binding)
1. Stegosaurus — Juvenile literature. I. Title.
QE862.O65 T46 2015
567.915—d23

Published in 2015 by
Gareth Stevens Publishing
111 East 14th Street, Suite 349
New York, NY 10003

Designer: Nicholas Domiano
Editor: Ryan Nagelhout

Illustrations by Jeffrey Mangiat
Science Consultant: Philip J. Currie, Ph.D., Professor and Canada Research Chair of Dinosaur Palaeobiology at the University of Alberta, Canada

Printed in the United States of America

CPSIA compliance information: Batch #CW15GS: For further information contact Gareth Stevens, New York, New York at 1-800-542-2595.

Contents

Boldface words appear in the glossary.

The Roofed Lizard

The *Stegosaurus* was known for the bony plates on its back. Its name means "roofed lizard." At first, scientists wrongly thought its plates lay flat on its back like tiles on a roof! The *Stegosaurus* lived millions of years ago.

The *Stegosaurus*'s plates were shaped like leaves. They were used to keep it safe from **predators**. They could also be used to keep the dinosaur warm when the weather was too cold. Special **blood vessels** in the plates took in heat from the sun.

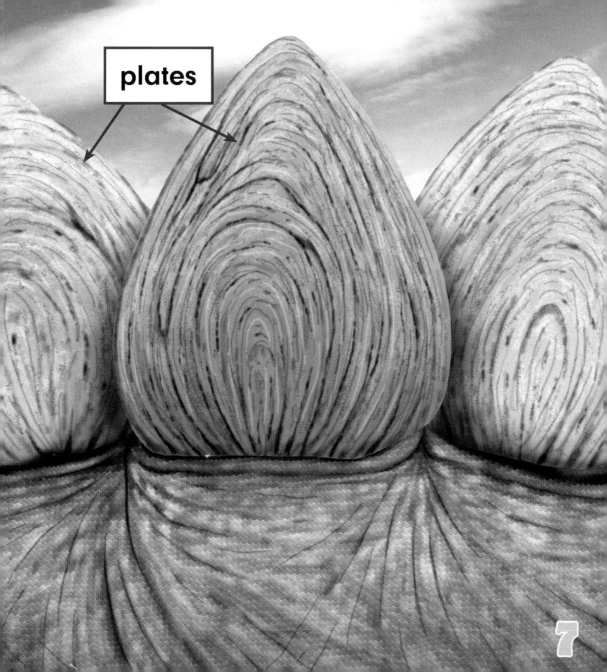

plates

7

A Terrifying Tail

To go along with the plates on its back, the *Stegosaurus* also had **spikes** on its tail! It could swing its tail back and forth very quickly. This made its tail useful for fighting off predators, which included large, meat-eating dinosaurs.

Time to Eat!

Stegosauruses were tough fighters. However, they weren't predators. They were herbivores, which means they ate only plants. They ate a lot of mosses and **ferns**. Do you like to eat fruits? If you do, you're like a *Stegosaurus!*

As Big as a Bus!

Stegosauruses had to eat a lot of plants because they were very big dinosaurs. A *Stegosaurus* could grow to be 12 feet (3.7 m) tall. It was also 30 feet (9 m) long, which is about as long as a bus!

13

Moving Slowly

A *Stegosaurus* weighed about 6,600 pounds (3,000 kg). It moved slowly on its four thick legs. It could only run about as fast as a person can. The *Stegosaurus* also had a small brain for being such a large dinosaur.

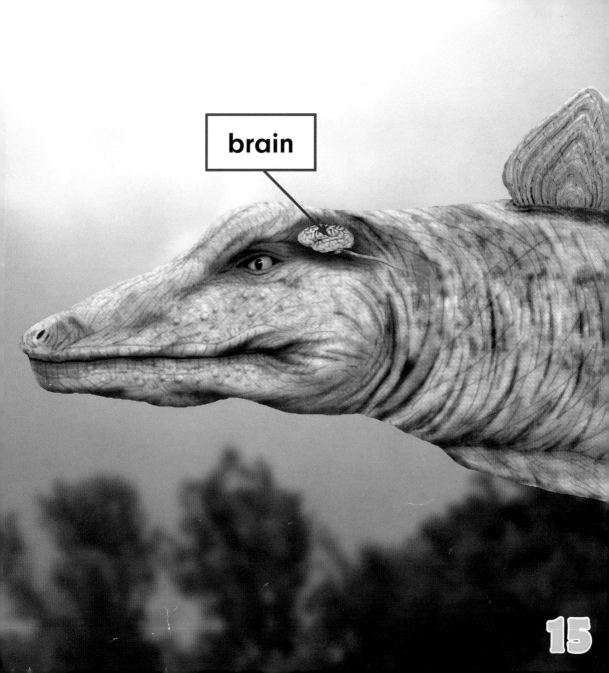

brain

Eggs and Babies

Scientists think *Stegosauruses* laid their eggs in nests they made on the ground. Then, baby *Stegosauruses* came out of the eggs. However, scientists don't know for sure if *Stegosauruses* built nests because they've never found *Stegosaurus* eggs.

A North American Dinosaur

Studying *Stegosaurus* **fossils** helps scientists learn about where these dinosaurs lived. Many *Stegosaurus* fossils have been found in North America. Scientists believe these dinosaurs lived in areas that are now part of the United States, including Oklahoma, Colorado, and Utah.

Fossil Finds

You can see *Stegosaurus* fossils in science **museums** around the world. The first *Stegosaurus* fossil found outside of North America was discovered in Portugal in 2007. This led scientists to believe that *Stegosauruses* may have walked across a land bridge from North America to Europe!

Glossary

blood vessel: a small tube that carries blood to different parts of an animal's body

fern: a type of plant that has large leaves and no flowers

fossil: the hardened remains of an animal or plant that lived long ago

museum: a building in which things of interest are displayed

predator: an animal that hunts other animals for food

spike: a long, pointy body part

For More Information

Books

Alpert, Barbara. *Stegosaurus*. Mankato, MN: Amicus, 2014.

Raatma, Lucia. *Stegosaurus*. Ann Arbor, MI: Cherry Lake Publishing, 2013.

Silverman, Buffy. *Can You Tell a Stegosaurus from an Ankylosaurus?* Minneapolis, MN: Lerner Publications Company, 2013.

Websites

Dinosaurs Quiz
kids.discovery.com/quizzes/animals/dinosaurs-quiz
Test your knowledge of facts about *Stegosaurus* and other dinosaurs by taking this quiz.

Stegosaurus
walkingwithdinosaurs.com/dinosaurs/detail/stegosaurus/
The website for the *Walking with Dinosaurs* movie and live show features many fun facts about *Stegosaurus* as well as other dinosaurs.

Index